The Art of Crafting AI Prompts

5

Introduction

In today's rapidly evolving technological landscape, artificial intelligence (AI) and language models have taken center stage, transforming the way we interact with machines and the digital world. Among the many fascinating aspects of AI, prompt engineering emerges as a crucial and intricate art that guides AI language models to produce accurate, creative, and contextually relevant responses.

What is Prompt Engineering?

At its core, prompt engineering is the craft of designing and fine-tuning precise instructions, known as prompts, to shape the behaviour of AI language models. These prompts act as input cues, influencing the language model's responses, and allow us to harness the full potential of these powerful AI systems.

The Importance of Prompting in AI Language Models

The significance of prompt engineering cannot be overstated. In the world of AI, the right prompt can make all the difference between generic and tailored responses. A well-crafted prompt empowers AI language models to provide contextually appropriate answers, understand user intent, and excel in a wide range of tasks such as chatbots, language translation, question-answering systems, and more.

Understanding the Scope of This Book

"The Art of Crafting AI Prompts: A Step-by-Step Guide" sets out to unravel the intricacies of prompt engineering, equipping readers with the knowledge and skills to become proficient prompt engineers. From beginners eager to embark on their AI journey to seasoned practitioners seeking to refine their craft, this book accommodates all skill levels.

Throughout these pages, we delve into the foundations of AI language models, explore the various prompt engineering techniques, and showcase real-world applications. From template-based prompts to machine learning-based approaches, readers will uncover a diverse set of tools and strategies that can be applied to shape AI's language in exciting and innovative ways.

Moreover, this guide emphasises the ethical considerations that come with prompt engineering, ensuring responsible and unbiased use of AI technology. Practical exercises and projects offer readers the opportunity to apply their knowledge hands-on, fostering a deeper understanding of prompt engineering principles.

Join us on this captivating journey into the heart of prompt engineering, where creativity meets technology and the possibilities of AI language models are truly unleashed. Let's embark together on this empowering exploration, paving the way for a future where AI speaks with clarity, precision, and human-like understanding.

In this section, we lay the essential groundwork for prompt engineering, exploring the core principles and concepts that underpin the art of crafting effective prompts for AI language models.

The Basics of AI Language Models

Before delving into prompt engineering, it's crucial to understand the fundamentals of AI language models. We introduce readers to the architecture and workings of these sophisticated systems, explaining how they process and generate human-like text.

How Prompts Influence Model Outputs

The heart of prompt engineering lies in comprehending the profound influence prompts have on AI language model outputs. We explore the intricate relationship between input prompts and the subsequent responses generated by the model, showcasing how even subtle changes in prompts can result in vastly different outcomes.

Types of Prompting Techniques

Prompt engineering offers a diverse array of techniques to mould AI language model behaviour. In this section, we examine the three primary categories of prompting techniques: template-based prompts, rule-based prompts, and machine learning-based prompts. Each approach possesses unique strengths and applications, empowering prompt engineers to adapt their strategies to various tasks and scenarios.

Throughout this foundational exploration, readers will gain a solid understanding of AI language models and their interaction with prompts. Armed with this knowledge, they will be well-prepared to embark on the journey of crafting AI prompts that shape the future of AI-powered language processing.

Keywords: Unlocking the Power of Prompt Engineering

Keywords play a pivotal role in prompt engineering, serving as strategic cues that guide AI language models to execute specific tasks or generate targeted responses. These carefully chosen words trigger the model's capabilities, influencing its behaviour in profound ways. Let's explore a diverse range of keywords and their applications, empowering prompt engineers to craft prompts that extract the desired outputs.

Write

Write Example: "Write a blog post about the benefits of mindfulness in the workplace."

The "Write" keyword instructs the AI language model to generate a piece of content, such as an article, blog post, or essay, centred around the specified topic. This allows users to leverage AI to create informative and engaging content quickly.

Classify

Classify Example: "Classify the products into three different price ranges: budget, mid-range, and premium."

The "Classify" keyword prompts the AI language model to categorise items or objects into distinct groups based on specified criteria. It is useful for organising and sorting data efficiently.

Summarise

Example: "*Summarise the main findings of the research paper on renewable energy sources.*"

The "Summarise" keyword directs the AI language model to condense a lengthy document or article into a concise overview of its main points. This enables quick access to essential information and aids in research and data analysis.

Translate

Example: "*Translate the conversation from English to Spanish.*"

The "Translate" keyword empowers the AI language model to provide accurate translations between languages, facilitating cross-cultural communication and global accessibility.

Order

Example: "*Order the list of movies based on their release dates from oldest to newest.*"

The "Order" keyword instructs the AI language model to arrange items or elements in a specific sequence based on given criteria. It assists in sorting data in a logical and structured manner.

Analyse

Example: "*Analyse the sales data and identify trends in customer preferences.*"

The "Analyse" keyword prompts the AI language model to examine data, charts, or graphs and derive meaningful insights, enabling data-driven decision-making and deeper understanding of trends.

Compare

Example: "*Compare the features of two smartphones and recommend the best choice.*"

The "Compare" keyword guides the AI language model to evaluate and contrast the attributes of two or more items, aiding users in making informed choices.

Contrast

Example: "*Contrast the pros and cons of working remotely versus working in an office.*"

The "Contrast" keyword instructs the AI language model to analyse and highlight the positive and negative aspects of different options, assisting users in weighing their options.

Evaluate

Example: "*Evaluate the marketing campaign's success in increasing brand awareness.*"

The "Evaluate" keyword prompts the AI language model to assess the performance and impact of a specific strategy or approach, facilitating data-backed assessments.

Explain

Example: "*Explain the principles of blockchain technology to a non-technical audience.*"

The "Explain" keyword guides the AI language model to communicate complex concepts or topics in a clear and easily understandable manner, making it valuable for educational purposes.

Generate

Example: "*Generate creative ideas for team-building activities.*"

The "Generate" keyword empowers the AI language model to produce a range of ideas, solutions, or options to address a specific problem or challenge, fostering innovation and creativity.

Identify

Example: "*Identify the primary causes of low employee satisfaction.*"

The "Identify" keyword directs the AI language model to pinpoint the primary factors or causes related to a particular issue or situation, aiding in problem-solving and decision-making.

Infer

Example: "*Infer the definition of 'ephemeral' in the given context.*"

The "Infer" keyword guides the AI language model to deduce the meaning of a word or concept based on the provided context, enhancing language comprehension and interpretation skills.

Predict

Example: "*Predict the sales growth for the next quarter.*"

The "Predict" keyword prompts the AI language model to forecast future trends or outcomes based on historical data or patterns, assisting businesses in planning and strategizing.

Recommend

Example: "*Recommend the most suitable laptop for graphic design.*"

The "Recommend" keyword empowers the AI language model to suggest the best option or solution based on specified criteria, facilitating decision-making processes.

Rephrase

Example: "*Rephrase the following sentence: 'The weather is nice today.*"

By using Rephrase in prompts, prompt engineers can expand the range of possible outputs and enhance the naturalness and diversity of the AI language model's responses

Simplify

Example: "*Simplify the explanation of quantum mechanics for high school students.*"

The "Simplify" keyword guides the AI language model to present complex concepts or information in a clear and accessible manner, making it easier for diverse audiences to understand.

Synthesize

Synthesize Example: "*Synthesise data from various surveys to form a comprehensive report.*"

The "Synthesize" keyword instructs the AI language model to combine information from multiple sources or datasets to create a cohesive and comprehensive analysis, assisting in data synthesis and report generation.

By skillfully incorporating these keywords into prompts, prompt engineers empower AI language models to perform an array of tasks and deliver tailored responses. These strategic cues optimise the efficiency and effectiveness of prompt engineering, making the AI interaction experience more productive and enlightening. The judicious use of keywords is a cornerstone of prompt engineering, paving the way for seamless interactions with AI language models across diverse domains and applications.

The Fundamentals of Prompt Structure

A prompt can encompass various components, with their arrangement tailored to achieve specific outcomes. Whether seeking informative responses, contextually relevant replies, or action-oriented results, prompt engineers can leverage a diverse combination of elements. Here, we explore the building blocks of a prompt, offering insights into their potential arrangements:

Instructions

Instructions form the core of a prompt, explicitly guiding the AI language model's intended action or response. They serve as the compass, steering the model towards the desired outcome. Depending on the task, instructions can be straightforward or elaborate, directing the model to answer questions, provide recommendations, or generate creative content.

Example: Instruction: *"Compose an engaging marketing email to promote our latest product."*

Context

Contextual information enriches prompts, furnishing AI language models with additional data to respond more intelligently and accurately. By providing context, prompt engineers can shape the model's understanding of the query and influence the tone, style, or depth of the generated output. Contextual cues set the stage for more personalised and context-aware interactions.

Example: Context: *"You are the customer support representative for a tech company. The user is inquiring about their order status."*

Input Data

Integrating input data into a prompt empowers AI language models to perform actions or processes on the provided information. From numerical values to text inputs, incorporating data into prompts allows users to receive dynamic and relevant responses. Input data enables AI language models to generate customised recommendations, calculations, or task-specific outputs. Example: Instruction: *"Calculate the total revenue for the quarter using the following sales figures: [data]." Input Data: "Sales figures: $25,000, $30,000, $40,000"*

Output Indicator

Output indicators act as guiding labels or tags, prompting AI language models to respond in specific ways. By including output indicators, prompt engineers can influence the model's behaviour towards generating responses aligned with desired attributes, such as sentiment, tone, or formality. Output indicators are particularly valuable in ensuring consistency and adherence to predefined guidelines.

Example: Instruction: "*Compose a formal response to the customer complaint with a positive and empathetic tone*." Output Indicator: "Formal and Empathetic Response"

24

Role Prompting: Guiding AI with Contextual Role-Based Instructions

Role prompting is a powerful technique in prompt engineering where the AI language model is provided with context about its assumed role or identity. By setting the model into a specific role, such as a teacher, a doctor, or a customer service representative, prompt engineers can constrain the model's responses within the expected knowledge domain of that role. This contextual framing ensures that the AI generates responses appropriate to the designated persona, enabling more focused and relevant interactions.

Example: "*Act like you are an environmental scientist conducting a presentation on climate change to a group of students. Explain the greenhouse effect in simple terms?*"

In this example, the AI language model is primed to respond as if it were an environmental scientist addressing young students. The explanation about the greenhouse effect will be presented in a manner suitable for the audience's comprehension level.

Zero-Shot Prompting: Filling in the Blanks with Single Instructions

Zero-shot prompting involves providing the AI language model with a single set of instructions, a statement, or a question without any specific training examples. This technique challenges the model to generate meaningful responses without explicit prior exposure to the exact task, showcasing its ability to generalise knowledge.

Example: *"Compose an email inviting friends to a barbecue party this weekend."*

With only this prompt, the AI language model creates an original email inviting friends to a barbecue party, demonstrating its ability to generate coherent and contextually appropriate content based on the given instruction.

One-Shot Prompting: Guiding Responses with a Single Example

One-shot prompting provides the AI language model with a single prompt and response example, serving as a priming mechanism for the model to generate similar structured responses. The model leverages this example to align its outputs with the given response format.

Prompt: "Review: The customer service was excellent, and the product exceeded my expectations. - Los Angeles, CA" Response
Example: "Sentiment: Positive"

Using this one-shot prompt, the AI language model deduces the expected format for providing sentiments based on the given review example, and then generates sentiments for subsequent reviews accordingly.

Few-Shot Prompts: Limited Context for Enhanced Responses

Few-shot prompting entails providing the AI language model with a small number of examples to guide its responses. This approach is useful for training models to understand specific patterns or tasks with minimal training data.

Example:
Translate the following phrases from English to Spanish:
"Hello, how are you?"
"Goodbye and take care."
"Can you help me, please?"

Chain-of-Thought (CoT) Prompting: A Step-by-Step Approach

Chain-of-Thought (CoT) prompting involves presenting the AI language model with a series of prompts in a sequential manner, where each prompt builds on the previous ones.

This method guides the model's thought process, allowing it to reason step-by-step and generate coherent responses.

> Example:
> *Prompt: "Describe the life cycle of a butterfly."*
> *Model's Response: "A butterfly starts as an egg, hatches into a caterpillar, undergoes metamorphosis in a chrysalis, and finally emerges as a beautiful butterfly."*
> *Prompt: "Explain the importance of pollination in plant reproduction."*
> *Model's Response: "Pollination is crucial for plant reproduction as it enables the transfer of pollen from the male to the female reproductive organs, leading to fertilisation and the production of seeds."*

By employing role prompting, zero-shot prompting, one-shot prompting, few-shot prompting, and chain-of-thought (CoT) prompting, prompt engineers can efficiently guide AI language models to produce contextually appropriate, accurate, and informative responses. These techniques harness the full potential of prompt engineering, revolutionising the realm of natural language processing and enabling AI to excel in diverse applications and domains.

Evaluating and Iterating Prompt Performance

In prompt engineering, the process of crafting effective prompts does not end with their initial creation. Evaluating and iterating on prompt performance is a crucial step to refine and optimise AI language model interactions. Prompt engineers must continuously assess how well the prompts elicit desired responses and align with user expectations. This iterative approach enables prompt engineers to fine-tune prompts, improve AI model behaviour, and enhance the overall user experience.

The Importance of Evaluation

Evaluating prompt performance is essential to gauge the effectiveness of prompts in achieving their intended objectives. By assessing the quality and relevance of the generated responses, prompt engineers can identify strengths and weaknesses in the prompt structure, context, and usage of keywords. Effective evaluation leads to actionable insights, guiding prompt engineers to make informed decisions for prompt refinement.

Methods of Evaluation

There are several methods prompt engineers can employ to evaluate prompt performance:

> **Human Evaluation**: Human evaluators play a pivotal role in assessing the quality of AI-generated responses. By soliciting feedback from human users, prompt engineers can understand how well the responses meet user expectations and whether they align with the intended use case.
>
> **Automated Metrics**: Automated metrics, such as accuracy, fluency, coherence, and relevancy, can provide quantitative insights into the model's performance. These metrics offer a standardised way to measure the AI language model's output against a set of predefined criteria.
>
> **Comparison with Baselines**: Comparing prompt-engineered outputs with baseline responses or alternative prompt formulations helps identify which prompts lead to the most desirable results. This comparison assists in discerning the impact of prompt modifications on model behaviour.

Addressing Prompt Challenges

During the evaluation process, prompt engineers may encounter challenges, such as biassed responses, overgeneralization, or underperformance in specific contexts. Addressing these challenges requires an iterative and creative approach, wherein prompt engineers experiment with different prompt structures, context framing, and keyword usage to find optimal solutions.

Iterative Refinement

Based on the evaluation results, prompt engineers iteratively refine prompts to enhance their performance. They may adjust the wording, context, or keyword selection to elicit more accurate and contextually appropriate responses. The iterative process involves a continuous feedback loop, ensuring that the prompt-engineered outputs consistently align with user needs and expectations.

User Feedback Integration

User feedback serves as a valuable resource for prompt engineers. Incorporating user feedback into the iterative process helps prompt engineers gain insights into user preferences, pain points, and areas for improvement. This user-centric approach fosters the creation of prompts that resonate better with the user base.

Evolving with Model Updates

As AI language models evolve through updates and fine-tuning, prompt engineers must adapt and reassess prompt performance. Ensuring that prompts remain effective with the latest model versions guarantees consistent high-quality interactions.

By embracing a data-driven, iterative, and user-focused approach to evaluating and refining prompt performance, prompt engineers unlock the true potential of prompt engineering. This continuous improvement process strengthens the symbiotic relationship between AI language models and prompt engineers, leading to more seamless, contextually-aware, and engaging AI-powered interactions.

Addressing Challenges and Pitfalls

Prompt engineering is a dynamic and evolving field that comes with its own set of challenges and pitfalls. As prompt engineers strive to create effective prompts for AI language models, they must be vigilant in addressing these challenges to ensure optimal performance and ethical considerations. Let's explore some common challenges and how prompt engineers can navigate them:

Common Mistakes in Prompt Design:

Ambiguity

Ambiguous prompts can lead to unpredictable or irrelevant responses from AI language models. To avoid this, prompt engineers must strive for clarity and specificity in their instructions, leaving little room for misinterpretation.

 Example: Ambiguous Prompt - "*Write a story about a man and his dog.*"

Better Prompt - "*Compose a heartwarming tale about a man who adopts a rescue dog and their adventures together.*"

Bias Reinforcement

Prompts that inadvertently reinforce biases present in the training data can result in biased AI outputs. Prompt engineers should carefully curate and diversify prompt examples to avoid perpetuating societal biases.

Example: Biased Prompt - "*Describe a successful CEO.*"

Unbiased Prompt - "*Describe a visionary leader who has achieved success in their respective field.*"

Overcoming Data Limitations

Lack of Domain-Specific Data

In specialised domains, obtaining a sufficient amount of high-quality data can be challenging. Prompt engineers can explore data augmentation techniques or leverage transfer learning from pre-trained models to address this limitation.

Data Imbalance

Skewed data distributions can lead to biassed AI language model outputs. To mitigate this, prompt engineers should strive to balance and diversify the training data to avoid over-representing certain patterns or categories.

Example: In sentiment analysis, ensuring an equal number of positive, negative, and neutral sentiment examples in the training data prevents bias towards any particular sentiment.

Ethical Considerations in Prompt Engineering

Fairness and Inclusivity

Prompt engineers must ensure that prompts and AI language models uphold principles of fairness and inclusivity, avoiding the amplification of harmful stereotypes or exclusionary language..

Privacy and Confidentiality

Prompts that inadvertently lead to the disclosure of sensitive information should be avoided. Prompt engineers must prioritize user privacy and confidentiality in interactions with AI language models.

Providing explanations for the AI language model's outputs can build trust with users. Prompt engineers should strive for transparency in the prompt design to foster a clearer understanding of how AI-generated responses are produced. Example: Including a request for the model to provide justifications for its answers when appropriate.

By proactively addressing challenges and considering ethical implications, prompt engineers can cultivate responsible and robust prompt engineering practices. Embracing a user-centric and ethically-minded approach strengthens the positive impact of AI language models, fostering trustworthy and valuable interactions in various applications and domains.

Real-World Applications of Prompt Engineering

The fusion of prompt engineering techniques with cutting-edge AI tools like ChatGPT has revolutionised industries and transformed human-AI interactions. Let's dive into some remarkable real uses of prompt engineering in various domains :

Customer Support and Service:

Enhancing Customer Interactions Example:
"*As a customer support representative for TechGenius, help the user troubleshoot internet connectivity issues with their modem. Ensure the response includes step-by-step instructions to check cables, reset the device, and test the connection.*"

In this scenario, prompt engineering enables AI language models to function as empathetic virtual customer support agents. Prompt engineers carefully craft context-aware prompts to guide the AI language model's responses, facilitating smooth and informative interactions with customers seeking assistance. AI-powered virtual agents can handle customer queries, track orders, and provide product information, streamlining the customer support process and enhancing the overall experience.

Healthcare and Medical Assistance:

Assisting Medical Professionals Example:
"*As a medical assistant, analyse the patient's symptoms, medical history, and provide a preliminary diagnosis for the skin condition. Suggest recommended treatments for further evaluation.*"

In this domain, prompt engineering plays a crucial role in guiding AI language models to support medical professionals. AI assistants can assist in diagnosing skin conditions based on symptoms and images, offering medical insights for preliminary analysis. Prompt engineers create prompts to ensure the AI's responses provide accurate and reliable guidance to healthcare providers and patients alike.

Personalized Educational SupportExample:
 "*As a virtual tutor, explain the concept of photosynthesis to a high school student in simple terms.*"

Prompt engineering enables AI language models to function as valuable educational aids. By crafting prompts that guide the AI in providing tailored explanations, students receive personalised support in understanding complex topics. Virtual tutors can offer explanations in a way that resonates with the student's level of understanding, fostering a more engaging and effective learning experience.
Content Creation and Copywriting:

Enhancing Content Creation Example:
 "*Compose a captivating blog post about sustainable living practices.*"

Prompt engineering empowers AI language models to assist content creators in generating engaging and original content. Writers can prompt AI models to write to diversify their portfolio."

Prompt engineering allows AI language models to provide personalised financial advice and analysis. Users can receive tailored recommendations for budgeting, investment opportunities, and risk assessment, empowering them to make informed financial decisions.

Legal and Compliance Assistance

Streamlining Legal Guidance Example:
 "As a legal assistant, explain the key points of the contract to the user."

In the legal domain, prompt engineering enables AI language models to assist in providing initial legal guidance and contract reviews. The AI responds with clear and concise explanations of legal terms, making the legal process more accessible and efficient.

Creativity and Storytelling:

Fueling Creative Narratives Example:
"Help me develop a captivating plot twist for my mystery novel."

Prompt engineering inspires creativity, turning ChatGPT into an interactive storytelling partner. Authors can prompt AI models to provide plot ideas, character development, and even unexpected twists, enriching the storytelling process.

These real-world applications of prompt engineering, powered by the versatility of ChatGPT, showcase the transformative impact of this technology across diverse industries and domains. From enhancing customer support to assisting medical professionals, fostering education, and enabling seamless cross-cultural communication, prompt engineering with ChatGPT has reshaped the way we interact with AI language models. The possibilities for future applications are boundless, promising continued advancements in AI technology and prompt engineering blog posts, social media updates, and marketing materials, tailored to their unique styles and target audiences. This application streamlines content creation and enhances marketing efforts across industries.

The Future of Prompt Engineering

Prompt engineering is a rapidly evolving field, poised to

shape the future of AI language models and their

applications. As technology continues to advance, the role of prompt engineers becomes increasingly pivotal in maximising the potential of AI-powered interactions. Let's explore the future of prompt engineering, including emerging trends and technologies, the challenges and opportunities that lie ahead, and a glimpse into the future of AI language models.

Emerging Trends and Technologies

Context-Aware Prompts

The future of prompt engineering will see a surge in context-aware prompts that enable AI language models to better understand user intent and provide more personalised responses. These prompts will leverage user history, preferences, and real-time interactions to enhance the user experience.

Multimodal Prompts

Prompt engineers will explore incorporating multimodal inputs, such as images, videos, and audio, to enrich interactions with AI language models. Multimodal prompts enable more comprehensive understanding and generation of content across various media types.

Transfer Learning for Prompt Engineering

Advancements in transfer learning techniques will empower prompt engineers to leverage knowledge from pre-trained models effectively. This will streamline prompt engineering and enable the creation of specialised prompts with limited training data.

Prompt Adaptation

In the future, prompt engineers may develop adaptive prompts that dynamically adjust based on user feedback and context, ensuring a continuous improvement in the AI language model's responses.

Challenges and Opportunities Ahead

Bias Mitigation

As AI language models are applied in diverse real-world scenarios, addressing bias in prompts will remain a significant challenge. Prompt engineers will have the opportunity to pioneer solutions that minimise bias and promote fairness in AI-generated content.

Human-AI Collaboration

The future of prompt engineering will likely involve more collaboration between humans and AI language models. Prompt engineers can design prompts that facilitate seamless cooperation, leveraging the complementary strengths of both.

Ethical Considerations

As AI language models become increasingly sophisticated, prompt engineers will need to stay vigilant about ethical considerations. They must navigate complex ethical dilemmas and ensure that prompts adhere to responsible AI practices.

Scaling and Efficiency
Prompt engineers will encounter challenges in scaling prompt engineering techniques to handle large-scale AI language models efficiently. Finding ways to optimise prompt design for performance and resource utilisation will be essential.

A Look into AI Language Models' Future

As prompt engineering continues to advance, AI language models will become more adept at understanding and responding to human inputs. They will seamlessly integrate into various industries, revolutionising customer support, education, healthcare, creative writing, and more. The future of AI language models may witness human-like interactions, where prompt-engineered prompts lead to dynamic conversations, opening up exciting possibilities for human-AI collaboration.

Additionally, AI language models might evolve to be more transparent and explainable, enabling prompt engineers to design prompts that provide clear justifications for their generated responses. This transparency will build user trust and facilitate responsible AI usage.

Ultimately, the future of prompt engineering holds immense potential for transforming the way we interact with AI language models, making them indispensable tools for enhancing productivity, creativity, and knowledge-sharing in a rapidly evolving digital landscape. As prompt engineers continue to push the boundaries of AI language model capabilities, the future of prompt engineering promises to be a fascinating journey of innovation and discovery.

Conclusion

In this comprehensive guide, we embarked on a journey through the captivating world of prompt engineering—a realm where creativity, precision, and innovation converge to shape the interactions between humans and AI language models. From the very foundations of prompt engineering to the future possibilities that lie ahead, we explored the art of crafting AI prompts step by step, empowering readers to master this transformative skill.

We delved into the fundamental principles of prompt engineering, understanding how prompts can be tailored to guide AI language models with strategic keywords and contextual framing. Through template-based prompts, dynamic variables, and user input incorporation, we unlocked the versatility of prompts in generating personalised and informative responses. Real-world examples demonstrated the application of each prompt type in AI-powered chat interfaces, making the knowledge immediately applicable to various professional scenarios.

Aspiring prompt engineers gained insight into the importance of context-aware prompts, where AI language models respond with tailored precision to specific roles, tasks, or scenarios. Zero-shot prompting showcased the incredible ability of AI models to generate responses with minimal explicit training, while one-shot and few-shot prompting offered efficient ways to guide model behaviour with concise examples.

We explored the art of word rephrase, expanding the creative boundaries of prompts and fostering diverse language patterns. Furthermore, we emphasized the crucial role of evaluating and iterating prompt performance, ensuring the continuous improvement of AI language model interactions. Addressing challenges and ethical considerations became paramount in responsible prompt engineering, safeguarding against biases and promoting fairness and inclusivity.

Finally, we gazed into the future of prompt engineering, witnessing emerging trends like context-aware prompts, multimodal inputs, and prompt adaptation that will shape the next generation of AI language models. Challenges and opportunities lie ahead, urging prompt engineers to pioneer solutions that align AI language models with human values and aspirations.

As we conclude this journey, we invite you to embrace the art of crafting AI prompts with confidence and creativity. Whether you are a seasoned AI professional or an aspiring prompt engineer, this guide equips you with the knowledge and tools to shape the future of AI language models. As AI continues to transform the way we live, work, and interact, prompt engineering stands at the forefront, empowering us to unlock the boundless potential of artificial intelligence, one prompt at a time. So, go forth, craft your prompts, and unleash the power of AI language models to make a positive impact in the world. The art of prompt engineering awaits your masterpiece.

Sources and References

Throughout the creation of "Empowering Human-AI Conversations: The Art of Crafting AI Prompts," we have drawn upon a wide range of sources and references that have enriched our understanding of prompt engineering and AI language models. The collective knowledge from these reputable sources has shaped the content and insights presented in this book. We express our gratitude to the following references for their valuable contributions:

OpenAI Research Papers:
https://openai.com/research

Chain-of-Thought Prompting Elicits Reasoning in Large Language Models
https://arxiv.org/pdf/2201.11903.pdf

Large Language Models are Zero-Shot Reasoners
https://arxiv.org/pdf/2205.11916.pdf